ENTER INVISIBLE

Enter Invisible

Catherine Wing

Sarabande ▦ Books
LOUISVILLE, KENTUCKY

FIRST EDITION

Managing Editor
Sarabande Books, Inc.
2234 Dundee Road, Suite 200
Louisville, KY 40205

LIBRARY OF CONGRESS CATALOGING-IN-PUBLICATION DATA

Wing, Catherine, 1972–
    Enter invisible : poems / by Catherine Wing.— 1st ed.
       p.   cm.
    ISBN 1-932511-30-X (cloth. : alk. paper) — ISBN 1-932511-23-7
(pbk. : alk. paper)
    I. Title.
PS3623.I645E58 2005
811'.6—dc22   2005000852

13-digit ISBN 978-1-932-51130-7 (hc); 978-1-932-51123-9 (pb)

Cover image: Untitled, anonymous. Provided courtesy of the Thomas
Walther Collection.

Manufactured in Canada
This book is printed on acid-free paper.

Sarabande Books is a nonprofit literary organization.

Enter Invisible is the second title in The Woodford Reserve Series in
Kentucky Literature.

This project is supported in part by an award from the National
Endowment for the Arts. Partial funding has been provided by the
NATIONAL ENDOWMENT FOR THE ARTS Kentucky Arts Council, a state agency in the Commerce Cabinet,
with support from the National Endowment for the Arts.

620608

for CW & RK,
heartbeat & hoofbeat

Table of Contents

ENTER INVISIBLE

ENTER INVISIBLE

for Northrop Frye

So she says to me, "You be the heavy father and I'll be the
hayseed." And she's alright, better than, and it's dark and the
bar pretty empty so we start this courtship mockery over a
Bud and peanuts and the noise of the dishwasher. She's calling
me Alazon but I don't know who that is and if it means, say,
scoring later on, I'll take it. She's in black and I'm in button-
down blue. At some point, I can't remember when (did I order
dinner?), dinner arrives and I eat and get fat—fast. She
becomes my daughter but I still want to sleep with her. What
bar is this, I'm thinking? The bartender looking at me like I'M
the brainworm, a professional fool...and he's right, for quick
as whippets I've got long ears and a tail. Jackass, I think. Fool, I
think. And my conquest, my daughter, she's trained the
eyeball elsewhere—so—I'm drowning in it, beer and air, and I
pull the bartender down and whimper, "I'm just a woodland
fellow," but he says, "You are an ass, indeed."

BEAUTY: TO DO

10:00, 3:00, 7:00, feed the dragon.
Practice happy face, smile, no ugh.
Please march, as the drum bangs on.

For the garden, salt on the slugs,
And only Sundays to slack off.
Be, Beauty, Be! Don't lurk.

Remember B-12 for agony,
B-6 and C in case of heart ruckus.
Don't mention 100 years slumber, the rape, again.

Wipe your feet after trekking in briar muck.
Catch up with your lag.
Revitalize your too-tired luck.

Be charming to guests until they are gone.
In case of a fire, call for a fire truck.
When the Prince is around, make sure to be on.

From THE GOLDEN BOOK OF SCIENCE
FOR BOYS AND GIRLS: an Introduction to Earth,
Sea—the Air—Plants, Animals, Man and His Inventions

After we define old, big,
far, fast, and hot
we get a million
kinds of animals—furred, feathered
or finned.
What a backbone is and
who has one, Chapter 10, page 20.

We look deep sea
and small silkworm
before moving on to inanimate
if alive. Sugar factories and
beggar plants followed by
flowers that we know and seeds
that go a-traveling.

By Chapter 21
we are ready for ourselves:
body, kneecap, small intestine;
what we eat, breath, and drink.
No surprises here,
until under our feet—fossils
reveal long ago

smolder and ice:
Ice Age and Old Faithful.

From down in wonder we turn
up to a-maze, Chapter 33,
above our heads
weather, cloud, and storm,
and higher still, sun, moon, and star,
then magnetism briefly, floating, flying,
light, shadow, and sound, pages 86–88.

An echo bounces through a jack-in-the-box
and light flickers in a kaleidoscope.
The periodic table blocks out
earth air fire water

where we pause—fire—
blessing before discovery—discovery—
page 95, Chapter 42.

THE GUST FRONT

In the headlong heart race
over the curve and spine of land
much coiffured cumulonimbus
heaped in heart rent
and mock rain flutter
moves vertical on
air currents along
and up lightning

Our hero in small prop
red baron of drought
flies through the keyhole
of cloud to deposit
starry ice-seedlings
lingers but a moment
in the billow enough
to uncorset untress
the cirrostratus tangle knot
and via striptease
seduce the cloud to rain

JOHNNY LOVE SONG

Johnny Ford come lately
and Johnny Donne come soon.
The two Johnnys gone round the world
dragging the weight of the moon.

The moon was in a pocket
and the pocket in his coat.
The coat was hung up by the door.
The door was on a boat.

Johnny Ford come lately
and Johnny Donne come soon.
The two Johnnys gone round the world
dragging the weight of the moon.

The moon said Johnny come here now;
the now said not today.
Johnny said I'll just be awhile;
the while turned into May.

Johnny Ford come lately
and Johnny Donne come soon.
The two Johnnys gone round the world
dragging the weight of the moon.

The moon and May took fancy;
fancy seasoned into love.
Johnny Ford and Johnny Donne
abandoned the moon above.

Johnny Ford come lately
and Johnny Donne come soon.
The two Johnnys gone round the world
dragging the weight of the moon.

TO THROW A WRENCH IN IT

Means we've gotten it wrong,
Hell is not a hidden place.
We mingle among mongrels.
Our footsteps leave no trace.

Leaving is a part of loving
And a wedding is a wager.
You are the wagon for your weight.
Sharp plus sour equals eager.

What's simple is usually folded.
A fever is not a favor.
Writing is about incision,
You can't erase it with a razor.

Our fate is bound to fatal.
It takes an era for some ore.
A fiasco moves beyond
The bottle it was born for.

We issue as we exit.
The daft man once was deft.
Your escape leaves you unbuttoned.
To remain will mean you left.

HAIL-FELLOW-WELL-MET

There is no such thing, he said.
There is no such other thing, he added.
That being the new way it was
I took a sip off my drink while a mermaid clung
to the glass at the edge of our conversation.
I also see ochre as oxblood, I replied, nodding vigorously.
The bar opened up then like a splash
of egg dye on water.
A roosting pigeon rushed by with the baling wire;
someone turned the sun down with a dimmer
and hung himself on the coat rack.
Oh, what a mess of antlers in the taxidermist's shop.
Have you seen Madame Damnable? Have you
seen the Inquisitor? Have you seen
static electricity in all these years?
We were all here a minute ago
figuring out the long side of a right triangle.
Given that sine over cosine plus z-sub-two
equals the firing squad, we are all in for it now.
The sun rounds the corner like a policeman in drag.
You are caught with your hands in the pockets
of your gabardine pants in a world where
red equals blue rivals green.
Sleep with it, the man says,
and you do.

DEAR SNOW,

The grandfather clock is set at bewilder
which means this tower spiraling
some un-time reads: if, when, awhile.

If the night hadn't come in like ink
against the castle's shore and briar isle,
then roses next, house and ingle.

But how are you and your worry wild?
And how's all that brood, short and short in sin,
excepting the basic grump, laze, hap. Wilt

come for Christmas, snowflake and spin?
Or are you still locked up a-wheel of wiles?
Damned stepmother washed up, has-been.

These days I have something of the guile
roosting under eave and shingle.
Dad, the king, looks at me and cries,

but I'm not hurt or bad beyond a splinter.
Harvest is in, the realm expanding and I
so-so in school. But he's gone mad to spindle.

(My advice is this:
Bewilder awhile wild eye and well,
splinter the spindle into spine, and ink and apple.)

Sigh,

Sleep

SOME HUMAN INCIDENT

After the baby we knew more, knew
Better, saw Kafka in the grillwork. An end to the
Cockleshell days, madeleines, pearlstones,
Duded up nights on the town. Hello Un–
Easy, dream barriers, briars in the cornstarch.
Foxholes appeared in the garden.
Genies went jitterbug, even the
Hawthorn was frantic. 70% of our town was
Inflammable, the rest ready as tinder.
Just as the bloom field was about to blow,
Ketchup catching on as a vegetable, the baby
Left, struck out for paradise on his own, with Teddy
Mounted in a bag on a stick.
Next, please, we shouted after him, but felt empty.
Oh, the deserts were just: a hollow
Palazzo, eggshells on the loudspeaker,
Queer baby ghosts that hovered at the periphery.
Right was wrong ever after.
Still, we thought he might come back
To us. We kept his room going,
Underscored his name on the mailbox.
Virtually every night we ate his favorite foods—
Wiener schnitzel and sauerkraut. Eventually
X replaced Y. We became him. We were where he got to.
You wouldn't understand. We don't. There's
Zip in the literature and we've looked it up.

THE STREAMLINED HEART

Might miss an ear,
Skip a beat,
Be too ready to ream,
Not choose to repeat,
Hard of hearing,
Or up a stream
(You can't streamline thread,
Earth's tinsel dream).

Reduced and
In parts—
I, am,
In and he
Toe the line,
Lack art.

TOM & JERRY GIVE CONTINUAL CHASE

Same is in and out and old. This sorrow
rinsed, wrung, and hung out to dry for tomorrow.

It's care that kills Mister Thomas Cat.
Whether blue ocean or black, *Muscat*

Beaumes de Venise by his side, or
Toodles feeding him grapes and idle

chatter, he dies. There are eighty-eight
modern constellations and five that circulate

without sinking below the earth's horizon.
It's Tom who Jerry's got his eyes on.

Despite it all, Tom knows the formula for a joke:
it's a noun, a verb, a yoke.

SAME OLD SAME OLD

Just back from a same old day
of work on a same old street.
The news repeats on the radio and I
eat from a jar of Spaghetti-Os—oh!
life! with the same old same old view.

The football game goes play-by-play.
On ER a dead man's wrapped in a sheet.
Captain Kirk hears Aye, Aye! Aye, Aye!
and that's the same old old
same thing now warped by something new.

Tick-tock, says the clock. We say, *Eh?*
The same-old's getting older. Now you see me,
tomorrow you won't. When we ask why
the answer is the same: old Death blows
on everyone—sad but true.

Tricky though because you have to wait
for him while he is either early
or late. The sun rises in the same old sky, the same old night
and moon, the same old stars that you don't know,
while an owl off in a field is whispering *Whoo?*

Meanwhile, dinner passes with me behind my TV tray.
The Sportscaster has cause to say "Sweeeeet!"

17

but I'm left sour and cold and dry.
Tomorrow's another day, you know.
Tomorrow will be different and new.

LOVE NOTE, LATE NIGHT GHAZAL

I love the night, the hat of every day.
—Vincente Huidobro

Behind the house and eaves tonight
A backward glance of ease tonight.

The harvest moon puts on her horns
And the sky blushes cerise tonight.

So sun and day at last upend
And light wears the chemise of night.

Lightning throws a switch
And there are stars in the valise of night.

If I were here and you were here
Together we'd appease the night.

If I were three and you were four
We'd be the Pleiades tonight.

Meet the corner of west and wild
And I'll be your sweet breeze tonight.

Take wind and wing—be off for flight,
Instead of the trapeze tonight.

HECUBA TO HIM

Dulcet—Dear,

We are gone beyond—behind—Fahrenheit.
The sun is done with rising, so just candlelight

and moon. I am of the February opinion
that we might never make it back, well *(bien)*,

before summer. Already I am on the eve
of a nagging joke with not one trick up my sleeve.

All my yucks are cracked and archived.
My chuckle is consumed—my ideas are tired.

Figaro's honed his daughter to a hardtack.
She works on little else but ice and cork.

Jim's inseminated a huge percentage of cockatoo,
yet none will bear an egg. And—guess who?—

even Bismuth's got the Peste. I am ashamed,
Bobbin, to admit our aeronautic fray

is at both ends of the knot. Even the chargeable
countdown has lost its charge.

Where's the whiteout for this brouhaha?
And you love, so far afield? acontinent? astar?

Spell me from this spell.
Please also send horsepower, fructose, groundswell.

All love,

the Player

COUNTING SONG #1

One legless bird of paradise unable
to land. Two feathers from the King Bird's lyre.
Three bees weaving your halo. Four twists of fate
and five beans, two in each hand and one in the mouth.
Six beams of light slowed to a tricycle's pace
traveling alongside you. Seven Siamese-twinned apples
suspended in amber. Eight hidden worlds in nine
microscopes. Ten cases curio and wanderlust.

TOM & JERRY *AU FEU LES POMPIERS*

That day in the funny paper the acrostic
had a message for Tom, a caustic

morsel, an acidic tidbit, clue #5: "Hey Catnip,"
it said, "Is your partner satisfied?" which planted a pin's tip

of doubt, gave operational pause, ushered in an ague
for Tom, and required a call to the Assistance League,

who pitched, and tossed, and roiled like indigestion
about the sky, unable to answer a single question,

or settle his score with Jerry, or assuage
what by now had become a paralyzing stage

fright and inability to perform, an elephantine
lack of the you-know-what-where and hell if

he knew what to do for it next,
where else to go or who else to hex,

and then life's little switchman Death came along
and offered him a bit of his stiffy for a song.

EVOLUTION SONG

The poison frog becomes the poison arrow
From a tadpole comes a toad
To the lungfish comes the land we're on
From the city comes the road

A milk-thief once made butterfly
A moth once lived in silk
The mayfly lives and dies in May
A bird was once an alligator's ilk

Those with spines will lose them
And those without will gain
A shell becomes your cover
From the water comes the rain

A hornworm ends as hawkmoth
In the muscle is a mouse
The egg tooth cuts the egg you're in
Your temple turns to house

FIVE NINETEEN-WORD AUTOBIOGRAPHIES

I

Anything pinball,
A little mazurka.
Only one of these answers is true.
Sea-wasp, skeleton-whisper.
Goodbye flying fisherman.

II

Sometimes the wind leaned on the sea,
Shifted its weight like fever.
Your letter lost in the letter box.

III

In a hall of mirrors
He played the mysterious stranger,
A fake-door trick-eye trick.
A one-liner.

IV

6,000 nights.
The devil's deal
Buried in a pigeonhole.

A dropsical heart dropped in on
An echo's empty shell.

V

Into this wonder cabinet,
Urbi et Orbi,
Ace of the Universe,
A billion to the billionth,
An inlet outletting.

I SAW U

Blue buzz—or
wing stroke—six hands wrung
until then—unseen—
un-supped.

RE: Fly
as he appears to Mr. Toad—
Blur is your best color
—stained wings
in silhouette—a pebble
for a body—and—
zot!—kiss!—the tongue
apprehends
the subject.

TOM & JERRY HOLD THEIR PARTS DOWN

Six o'clock at night in the Yoshiwara,
Jerry hires a hooker between bars.

A chipper little missy from the next cage
over, some mousy hole, out on a jag

and ready for catnip—read, a miracle.
Gooseberries or gunflint, Jerry's a manacle,

and to be fair, has manacled himself
to Tom, pull-tabs, and a shelf-life of gin.

"Get lost, Catnip," Jerry growls, "This rondeau
is over." A little death over everything, re-enter Tom Doe.

ROGER TORY PETERSON MEETS EDITH WHARTON BY CHANCE IN THE PASSAGEWAY

One night in the wide twilight belt of the Great Plains
with the accidentals gone home
and only that which was proper nestling down after dinner
to practice the agreed upon songs and calls,

Mrs. Ibis Linnet, formerly of —,
an old-fashioned, old-school nene,
sat at the foot of the dipper,
listening to poor-will and chuck-will's-widow,
judging the height of sound,
and waited for Barn Owl to come home.

Now on the other side of the water ouzel,
pining through bulrush and arrowleaf,
was Baldpated Bufflehead, hardly the Kingfisher
but comfortably set in sedge and smartweed
and a home by the sea.

How he loved her.

So, the collective sighs for mismatches and
blindness in love. I will say right now there are no
Buffleheaded Linnets at the end.

But this one night under flicker and swallow,
with full falcon and owl away,
the two met on the tow path.
There was nothing but an eider's touch,
the light of the bluethroat and nuthatch
calling "Towhee...Towhee..."
And this was enough
for the swan's loon into the nightjar.

EXCLAMATION

Halfway to the hemistich
> the chatterfly helicopters

To a quiver tempo.
> She quarries like quicksilver,

A garden overthrown
> with glitz and grammar.

Not for nothing
> do the gnats

Pool their passion
> for a shot at the superlative:

A shower of synonyms
> in the noun-dappled shade.

What a fluttering
> of affinity between flight

And float, commas
> of clamor and clover,

A genie dashed
> from a ginger jar.

Spring's varnish,
the verb's revolt,

Bounds towards
the bountiful in boldface.

In a word, full
of world: wonderful.

THE LAST HARANGUE AT THE GLACIER

The Ashman came as a Monk-Showboat.
Gallberry was served. Throughout the evening
giveaways seemed imminent. A certain Fleur-du-Mal
circled looking for anyone who might listen
to her loud-eater's monologue.
Oilseed was sent up to the King.
Wherever it was you got to,
you were missed. By 2 AM I was trapped
in a grammatic roundabout with a gaudy Chevalier
and his bleary Czech handkerchief.
Needless to say, there was a lot of insufferable dragging.

At last the Humboldt expert succeeded
in moving the earth and we were free to go.

TOM & JERRY TANGO

First, *walk:* Jerry filches Tom's thunder, pickpockets
his sockets clean, though the dance goes on clip-clop,

wig-wag. This beast has two tails, in accordance
with the music: *drag* and *push*. The accordion

pulls and *leans.* Second step: luck's unstruck by a stroke
(more like a slap) from God. Jerry's toe is trod,

third, *cut, cross,* and Tom's done it out of spite.
He wants his thunder back, *break, bite,*

but can't ask for it directly.
His smile is simply icing to his ire.

Fourth, lightning strike them both, *zig-zag,* a loss
for words. The music stops. Applause.

INTERMEZZO:
139 Words about Me

Dear Mr. Everything:
17 words about me. I like bad weather.
Seeking smarty-pants.
Drummers a plus.

❖

Dear Vanilla Pudding:
My pronunciation is often bad.
ISO the world's smallest parade.
No mullets.

❖

Dear Iniquitous Villain:
Kick my tires.
Seeking a synonym for nefarious.
Bad weather a plus.

❖

Dear Gentle Iconoclast:
For Sale... As Is.
ISO same.
No beef jerky.

❖

Dear Hey Sailor:
I'm an athletic drunk in an iron lung.
Need Deck Hand.
Usuals a plus.

❖

Dear Cute Punk Rock:
Tired of kicking.
Seeking similar bird of feather.
No hootchie-kootchie to start.

❖

Dear 17 Words:
Break me from my cancer shell.
ISO an iron lung.
Jesus a plus.

❖

Dear As Is:
The usual parade.
Seeking Latin Cosmonaut.
No discounts.

❖

Dear Dear:
I must stop somewhere.
ISO you.
The Universe, please.

THE EVIL HYPNOTIST PLANS HIS NEXT SESSION

Imagine,
your head is full of angry bees.
Your tongue is made of butter and
has melted. You are made of butter.
Now you are nothing but a stain on the carpet.

Imagine, please.
Your eyes are cocktail onions.
They cannot see.
Your lower half is planted in sand.
The tide is rising.

Imagine,
you are made of glass.
You are a candle snuffed.
A bubble blown—pop.
Don't breathe, please.

You are an old pickle jar
being filled with bacon grease.
A head full of dust, crumbs on a table.
You will be disposed of with a crumber.
Be still.

You are a hull of the unseaworthy.
You are the husk of the cicada,
the shell the snail abandons.
You are the bed of a stream
that's lost to drought.

Imagine, please.
A sandbag with a hole in it.
A slow leak.
A water balloon come undone,
empty and nothing until
you are dead.

You are dead.

THE PITCH

It's the story of a math genius posing as an imbecile or the one where Porky is saved from the slaughterhouse by a woman who wears no underpants. It's the story of a rapacious weed that takes over the earth, of One-Breasted Wanda falling in love with Jungle Jack. Ed Anger writes the story up. It's the story of a rash. And the story of a rash of deaths caused by a sea hag. It's the story of a woman who could not open her mouth and a woman who could not close her mouth. Maybe they meet. Maybe they don't. Maybe they are the perfect couple. It is the story of a man possessed by his tattoo. It's an exclusive. It's a curse or a commandment; it's a commandment on cursing which says for God's sake thou shalt not laze about on your chaise longue. It's a true story. It is the story of a man who talked his way out of credit-card debt. It is the story of the sunrise on July 10, 2003. It is the story of a traveling shadow. It is an old-man-walking-down-the-road story. It has a sculpted base to rest upon which can be yours if you act now.

COUNTING SONG #2

One day done for
bracketed by two long
nights and dark.
Third-time's charm is lost
and wrong. Repeat.
Four lies told and caught
up in five fights won
but at what cost?
Six songs are buried
in one dead lark.
Seven stories sold and bought
but eight nothings—
sweet or not—
will never be enough.
We'll want more
nine times—nine lives—
out of ten.
Ten fools fool
ten men.

JERRY FALLS FROM THE GRACE OF GOD

Granted that every gem has its flaw, the search
for which can reach

a full-time occupation, how many angles
on the garnet render it mere garnish? What angel

is in charge of that? Which backward alchemist
changes his gold into dung? And if the Acting

Mayor of your town condones it? What then?
Pills, guns, gas, or defenestration?

Tom's a fool and Jerry's too strong.
"That's not right," says Jerry. "You're wrong."

DEAR SLEEP,

Do you remember your friend Rapunzel?
Up in this stone tower in a sea of woods for
miles and ever and nary a puzzle

to play. Well, life's hard—not much lure,
lots of drag and muzzle.
But! Some prince was here, wasn't that a whir,

Some frolic and a little nuzzle.
I've never met one before and now all astir
I can hardly sleep to sleep for all the fuss.

He gave me a handful of aster
and while they're wilted now, I mull
them and him and I flush faster.

It's a strange ship we sail, heart against hull,
and you're right, he could be a bastard
but what do I know of kisses and swells?

He said my skin was white as alabaster,
and though I don't know what that is, it's Lady capital L!
Write me c/o Tower till June and Kingdom Come thereafter.

Spun,

Punzel

SPRINGTIME PREPARATION FOR WAR

Along 265-S between
Cosmosdale & Cementville—
Girls, Girls, Pool, and Pinball—
spring has reached up from the south
and taken hold of the county.
Everything is fluster and bloom.

In neighboring Fort Knox the tanks are out.
They echo low thunder that leans
toward the river. As the highway bends
and we round the corner
—helicopters! A flock of helicopters
has come to land in the valley!

THE WORLD'S MISERABLE CORNERS

Big Bang—Pause—Life.
Then man, nickel and dime,
Toupee.
Heartbreak, you bet. And man-of-war with his
Warships. Work-to-death camps—prefab-
Fabu!—and the coffin is free
(or cheap).
I say.
We've got it made.

COMMENTS FOR THE CZARINA

That night even the moon was living
in a puddle, a milky, watered-down
version of nightscape, flapping
its wings on the margins of murk.

Someone somewhere was
speaking of Cary Grant
in a restaurant dressed in voodoo lilies:
Vietnamien to L'Orangerie.

"Well," said our river-pirate, currently
writing a survival guide to small engines,
"It won't always be like buckshot
dropping in a bucket."

Meanwhile, a ways back
in the same line, a man was facing
a long commute in colloquial Bulgarian,
this rocket scientist with a

Wall Street focus to whom
someone was whispering, "Excuse me,
do you know the way
to the rickshaw dealership?"

Then five minutes of weather
and the melody of maritime
tragedy on the radio as
the clever-jack-chronicler,

who believes there is no one thing
to which everything corresponds,
cries out in his sleep,
"forbici, forbici, forbici."

PARADISE–UN

One of the early outline drafts of the poem [Paradise Lost] suggests that Milton was considering the alternative title "Adam Unparadized."

—Kevin Jackson, *Invisible Forms*

In the beginning God, unaccompanied,
And unmanned, made light.
Adam as yet unimagined.

Then the world unwound
From heaven. The day unbuttoned
From the night. The sea unearthed

And the earth unfastened
The grass and the trees unhusked
Their seeds. Adam unhastened.

God created He him, Adam unfallen,
Unpinned from the ground.
Unhitched Adam. Adam unbound.

And in order that Eve could uncage,
Adam unribbed, and both undressed
And were unashamed.

But the serpent (more subtle), unheard
From until now, unlocked and unappled
Eve, and Adam unabled.

Then the unthorned got thorns
And the unthistled thistles, the earth
Untoiled until then.

Adam unparadized—a song not
Unsung, of life's uneasying,
And Adam undone.

RIDDLE ON A NAY-WORD

Keep it. Zip it.
Don't utter a word
—mmm?

Not sure to what's referred?
This equation
Doesn't sum.

All jumbo mumbo,
Chance and choke,
The word's a code word, chum.

Sing it
As a butcherbird
Might hum.

Or the stumbling mumbler
Who leaves the joke half-heard,
Half ha-ha, half umm?

Or the mummer from the dumb show,
Quite dumb.
In a word—absurd.

Or your mother, mummy
—you're her third—
Singing sugar sugar sugar, plum.

A foreword and an after,
One crossword in the works
Means gum.

Between this catch and key
You're a blurréd whirlybird
And numb.

Perhaps, though,
The thought's occurred:
The word is mum.
Mum's the word.

POSTULATE

for CW

If a web's the spider's consequence,
      if water wears a skipped stone's name,
            then in me there is evidence of you.

If a slug leaves its route behind
      and a tire abandons its treads,
            then I wear a thread of you.

If cement can bear a handprint
      and the road ruts over time,
            then I am a hint of you.

If the wind pulls the weathervane,
      if the weathervane follows the wind,
            then here I strain for you.

If the shore marks a history of tides
      and the tides map the moon's longing,
            then I am occupied by you.

If love is visible in a face,
      if an expression casts a shadow,
            then in me see the trace of you.

COUNTING SONG #3

One static on the radio. Two bets
placed. Three airplanes circling overhead.
Four dogs howl at noon. Five
wheelbarrows carrying your load
as six fossil fish swim through the garden.
Seven stars caught in a cloud's bed. Eight suns
lost in space. Nine ambulances will save
you soon. Ten Tonka trucks rattle the road.

TOM TAKES THE CHEESE

It's midnight in the Derry-O.
Tom follows signs to water and air

while Jerry sleeps in his suicide
face. No matter—Tom's with the Swiss

Miss, and doesn't care. He has the startle
reaction of a stone, a boxer's 1000-yard stare.

And just as the new Ice Age starts its set
up in the Northern Hemisphere, Tom's coquette

gives over with a purr to the demands
of doggy style. Tom fancies himself a mantis

whose head's about to blow but
the reality is that he's a dribbler, a cut below

the rest. Welcome to the Invisibles Club, dear
Tom. We hope you'll like it here.

It's midnight in the Derry-O
and Jerry sleeps alone.

WALLACE TALKS TO STEVENS

SENSE: Poetry is the supreme fiction, Herr Doctor. Take the moral law and make a nave of it.

NON: It's hoo-hoo-hoo. It's shoo-shoo-shoo. It's ric-a-nic.

SENSE: It was when I said, "there is no such thing as the truth—"

NON: Said, "Phooey! Phoo!" She whispered, "Phui!"...the demi-monde on the mezzanine...said, "Phooey!" too, and a "Hey-de-i-do!"

SENSE: The particular question, here—

NON: *(interrupting)*. Pftt!

SENSE: The particular answer to the particular question—

NON: *(interrupting)*. Pftt!

SENSE: Is not in point—

NON: *(interrupting)*. Pftt!

SENSE: The question is in point.

Silence.

NON: Oh such tink and tank and tunk-a-tunk-tunk, Madame La Fleurie.

SENSE: *(angrily).* Yeah, add THAT to rhetoric.

NON: I sang a canto in a canton, Cunning-coo, O, cuckoo cock...rou-cou-cou.
He winks.

SENSE: I had as lief be embraced by the porter at the hotel as to get no more from the moonlight than your moist hand.

NON: *(rejected).* But the musky muscadines? The melons, the vermilion pears? *(Quiet. Defeated.)* Magnifico? Fabliau? *(Slow rising to crescendo.)* Orangeade?... Tea?!?! ...at the palaz of hoooon?

SENSE: *(disgusted).* One must have a mind of winter to regard the frost.

NON: *(equally disgusted).* O Remus...blow your horn.

SENSE: *(suddenly honest and sincere).* That's what misery is, nothing to have at heart. It is to have or nothing.

NON: *(still angry)*. Fat! Fat! Fat! Fat! ... as if the sun was blackamoor to bear your blazing tail.

SENSE: That's what misery is, nothing—

NON: *(snide, aside)*. Parl-parled the West-Indian weather.

SENSE: *(defeated)*. Nothing to have at heart.

NON: *(taunting)*. Teaching a fusky alphabet ... fusk-y fusk-y fusk-y.

SENSE: *(insistent)*. The house was quiet and the world was calm!

NON: *(ignoring SENSE, with his hands over his ears lalalala)*. Purple with green rings, or green with yellow rings, or yellow with blue rings.

SENSE: *(consoling herself with deep breathing)*. I am what is around me.

NON: *(more taunting)*. Pipperoo, pippera, pipperum ... the rest is rot.

SENSE: *(more deep breathing)*. Women understand this.

NON: *(taunting)*. Yillow Yillow Yillow Yillow Yillow Yillow.

SENSE: *(gaining, yelling).* One is not duchess a hundred yards from a carriage!

A long pause. Out of sheer frustration NON & SENSE *switch roles. All very quiet.*

NON: *(cowed).* What syllable are you seeking, Vocalissimus?

SENSE: *(crazed).* Mumbled zay-zay? and a-zay, a-zay? halloooo hallooo halloo?

NON: People are not going—

SENSE: *(interrupting).* To dream of baboons and periwinkles—

NON: *(interrupting).* Only, here and there, an old sailor, drunk and asleep in his boots—

SENSE: *(low whisper, lost).* Catches…tigers…in…red …weather.

(Silence. NON *is uncomfortable.* SENSE *has lost something.)*

NON: Well,…uhhh, good-bye Mrs. Pappadopoulos… and…uh, thanks.

❧ FIN ❧

TELL THEM

in response to John Stammers

Tell them all what you have done:
tell the sea and tell the sun;
the riptide as it carries off a child;
the weather, whether calm or wild;
gas attendants; postal clerks;
the priest; the president; the soda jerk.
Confess it quietly to recycling bins;
tell the sardines in their sardine tins.
Announce it to the media; swear it at the bar;
browse it in the library and translate near and far.
Declare it at the altar or on the witness stand.
Gather up your words and put them in your hands.
Watch them curse and chatter, break and betray.
They are no good at talking, no matter what they say.

STAR CHART

As if she had no alibi, no razz
backing up her dazz, no pitty-patty
carrying her tune in the world's jukebox.
Don Juan once beat her door down. Who knew
electricity came in such a pretty packet? The entire V
FD (Unit 36, Company 3) out of Kathmandu,
Georgia, fell for her while watching *What's Up Kitty Cat?*
Henceforth only kindling fires
instead of putting them out. Half heartbreaker-
jewel-thief, half high-muck-a-muck. Her IQ
killed a man—once. Now her up-n-up
leaned down-n-out. Her bravissimo
married some so-and-so and so the queenpin
nosedived into the gutter, more like a chasm
(or the Grand Canyon, she said, if it were in Hell).
Perhaps this story isn't new, the bright becoming berserk,
quicksilver silvering overly quick. It was she, shot J.
R. So beguiling was her fall from heaven they made a mini-
series about it—she played herself, nigh death,
to a T. The candle twice as bright burns only half as long
until it gutters out and dies from disbelief.
Venus to verboten in a single sentence.
What gives? How are we so easily misled?
X marks the spot, we're told, but it's at the bottom of the Pacific
—you're in cement shoes. And life, a hard heart throb,
zephyr-like, fails. Her last words were "Abracadabra."

DEAR PUNZEL,

Here we're all set to demolition,
More dust and qualm than midnight air.
We've danced the ball, and fired the musicians.

Everybody's on nails and needles, waiting to err.
Betray Queen's Edict, some mirrored position
With apples and huntsmen—I can't stand to be there.

And of your prince, fusion or fission?
First sight, fast stroke, did lightning dare?
Never mind, I've got a glass-box potion

Which will sell your soul and omit the bother,
Plunk you and your tower out by the ocean
With a milkmaid, manservant, and seven elder brothers.

It's a good life, maybe, no reason to shun
This luxury cottage for some castle or other.
The moon goes down and up comes the sun.

But let's face it, I'm living with dwarves and they smother.
And at present and in general, I'm feeling quite—un.
Just waiting for death by my wicked stepmother.

Sorry so glum,

White

A WEIGHT-BEARING SONG

You carry the fishwife and you carry her fish
You loft the anchor and its resting wish
The government wants you but your husband does not
You were the one whom the forget-me-not forgot

You don't get what's light, fire, or flash
You wonder why wood must burn to ash
You stole the gettin'—but the gettin' was gone
You away-ed to the edge but the edge had moved on

The alewife provides you with whiskey and gin
You dug the hole and it was you who fell in
You were the brood on which the broodmare stumbled
You were the hill down which Jill was tumbled

You pressured the man who felt his conscience times two
Then you peered in a puddle and saw it was you
You are the goose girl who shoulders the goose
You are the hangman who slipknots the noose

JERRY SHOOTS CRAPS

Jerry, being only a makeshift wiseacre,
living a life the size

of a spool of thread, can't afford
tolerance. He barbs wire from four

in the morning till close and then goes back
to eating peanuts. He hates the cat,

the dog, and the canary. He hates, in lieu
of what he is, what Tom has turned him into.

Most of all he hates this game he's always losing.
No, bitterness doesn't come close

to what he's got: a ball of muddied
yarn, a knotted heart that's died.

Tom, you must love Jerry.
Love him till your own heart is miscarried.

A SMALL PSALM

Sorrow be gone, be a goner, be forsooth un-sooth, make like a
suit and beat it, vamoose from the heavy heavy, be out from
under the night's crawlspace, call not for another stone, more
weight more weight, be extinguished, extinguish, the dark,
that which is deep and hollow, that which presses from all
sides, that which squeezes your heart into an artichoke-heart
jar and forbids it breathe, that which is measured by an
unbalanced scale, banish the broken, the unfixable, the
shattered, the cried-over, the cursed, the cursers, the curses—
curse them, the stone from the stone fruit, let it be fruit, the
pit from the pitted, the pock from the pocked, the rot from the
rotten, tarry not at the door, jam not the door's jamb, don't
look back, throw nothing over your shoulder, not a word, not
a word's edge, vowel, consonant, but run out, run out like the
end of a cold wind, end of a season, and in me be replaced
with a breath of light, a jack-o'-lantern, a flood lamp or fuse
box, a simple match or I would even take a turn signal, traffic
light, if it would beat beat and flash flood like the moon at
high tide, let it, let it, let it flare like the firefly, let it spark and
flash, kindle and smoke, let it twilight and sunlight, and
sunlight and moonlight, and when it is done with its lighting
let it fly, will-o'-the-wisp, to heaven.

MONEY-MAKING DOORKNOB HANGER ORDER FORM

Here's how it goes:
Our late luck late—you might say, overthrown—

We were at the edge of the season,
Ice & Cold Storage, heads full of bees, when

Voilà le Mannequin!
Out of the limberlost we moths, and into the echo machine

Which whisked us to the Café North Pole
For a One Size Missy and Shitzu Spangle singing "Olé!"

It wasn't enough to cast off the haunting,
Of course; the limelight was mere additive, a runt

Compared to moonlight, starlight, stoplight, lamplight, firefly.
But the Dragon-Wing-Remedy did serve briefly

To bring us from the devil. And then we were back to
Saying, "I might ought try to do it," then "alas," and finally
    "alack."

So we hung our heads and our hats on the sunset.
We had some fun, but we didn't make any money.

MONUMENT

Cast me from my devils.
Latch me to the sky.
Skip me like a stone over the surface of this duck pond.
Snap me like a switchblade.
Stretch me as a slingshot.
Throw me up like dust in a shaft of light.
Drench me in your downpour.
Put me on your compass.
Walk me through the cities of the dead.
Stitch me to your bones with sutures.
Run me through the hourglass.
Grind me into flour.
Whisper me from your songbook.
Keep my time in columns.
Add me to the ribs of your dome, and
arch my back.

MINI-SONNET

for CW

What?
When?
How?
Who?
That.
Then.
Now.
You.

Rain?
Heart?
Sea?
Chart.
Me.
Again.

FLOURISH. EXEUNT.

Here the moon plays catapult to cow.
The sky rewinds its batting back
To the horizon. Here it's Jill and Jack.

Here the clouds zip up the rain
And a ripple forms a raindrop.
We down hiccups. We swallow the baby.

Here a moth is born from fire
And it's the face that slaps down the hand.
The church spins down from the spire.

Here dynamite rouses the rubble
And a pinwheel pulls at the wind.
A clown inhales the bubbles

While the Piper—Pied—scatters
The children. And those who have died
Backpedal into life and matter

Greatly to the rest of us. Here
Where we take back our kisses
And pocket our handshakes.
Here where we edit the tide.

Acknowledgments

Many thanks to these journals in which the following poems (some in earlier versions) appeared:

Chicago Review: "Jerry Shoots Craps," "Tom Takes the Cheese"
Field: "Paradise-Un"
Fine Madness: "Roger Tory Peterson Meets Edith Wharton by Chance in the Passageway"
Hubbub: "Springtime Preparation for War"
MARGIE: "Beauty: To Do," "Flourish. Exeunt." under the title "In Reverse"
Poetry: "Evolution Song"
Prairie Schooner: "Comments for the Czarina," "Some Human Incident"

The Author

CATHERINE WING grew up in Louisville, Kentucky, on a street bounded by two florists, a cemetery, and a Carnegie library. She received her BA from Brown University and an MFA from the University of Washington. Her poems have appeared in such journals as *Chicago Review, Field* and *Poetry. Enter Invisible* is her debut collection.